Wandering Through the Fire

A Journey of Pain and Purpose

Volume 2- Transformation

Cyrus Cormier

ISBN: 978-1-945990-59-5

Published by High Tide Publications, Inc. www.hightidepublications.com

Thank you for purchasing an authorized edition of *Wandering Through the Fire - A Journey of Pain and Purpose - Volume 2 - Transformation.*

High Tide's mission is to find, encourage, promote, and publish the work of authors. We are a small, woman-owned enterprise that is dedicated to the author over 50. When you buy an authorized copy, you help us to bring their work to you.

Edited by Cindy L. Freeman

Book Design by Firebellied Frog Graphic Design www.firebelliedfrog.com

Foreword

Cyrus Cormier is a great person. I could stop right there and hear an overwhelming "Amen" from those who know him well. But that would not give the full picture of what makes Cyrus a great person.

Cyrus has always believed in having the best and giving his best. When I first met Cyrus in college he had the best car, best clothes, best attitude, and best work ethic. Nothing was given to Cyrus; he had the best because he gave his best to everything he did. I think we all had our time of backsliding in college, but for us, Cyrus was always the person of the moment. Everyone who knew Cyrus then, knew that, for him, the bigger the challenge, the bigger the effort. He had his career-best basketball game against Indiana State whose team included some guy named Larry Bird. Again, Cyrus poured out the best he had in himself.

Every year now we hold team reunions, and they are great times of sharing memories and having fun. But the emphasis is theme-centered on dedicating a large portion of our time and effort to feeding the homeless and visiting nursing homes in the community that gave so much to us.

Thanks to Cyrus, our reunions led us to create *The Twelve Plus One Heart Foundation* of which Cyrus is the president. Through the Foundation we were able to raise enough money to establish an endowment scholarship at NMSU that continues to help students in need of financial assistance.

Today we share a daily devotional that different members of our team send out to each other, another commitment that was birthed from our reunions. In these devotions we hold hope, we gain love, we seek HIS presence, and we pour out our heartfelt intentions.

All areas of Cyrus' life have been anchored and blessed by his spiritual faith and love for God. It is through this faith and love that he always gives his very best.

Over forty years ago, Cyrus introduced himself to me as Cyrus Cormier, but he added, "My friends call me Tip." He's been "Tip" to me ever since that day.

Greg "Spiderman" Webb

Former Teammate

Dedication

I give special recognition and dedication to Brandon Jamal Pate, who left us too soon but left us filled with hope and love. He was called B by those who knew and loved him. B, this is for you.

Bye, B

You left too soon,
I didn't say goodbye.
I look for you now
and all I do is cry.
You made me laugh,
you gave me hope.
I can't breathe and with
so much pain, I choke.
I hold your love
like I held your hand.
I pray to God that
in heaven is where you stand.
I look in the sky as
clouds pass me by,
I sit still and wonder
behind which one do you lie?
Our final goodbye
comes on this day,
In my heart forever,
my love for you will stay.

Contents

Guiding
Light

Forged by the Fire

Change is constant and never ending. As the Greek philosopher Heraclitus once said, "A man never steps in the same river twice." Both the river and the man constantly change. The dramatic transformation in my early twenties occurred as I endured and embraced fires on the journey of life. Enduring the pain and scars caused by hatred, I embraced faith and the reckoning of my soul. Enduring the challenges of skin color, I embraced authenticity. Enduring the grief of loss, I embraced love from both my family and random strangers. Enduring the sting of a flawed existence that was at times self-induced and at times induced by others, I embraced self-acceptance. Enduring the entirety of my brokenness, I embraced the lessons of silence and solitude.

It was when I recognized I was damaged but not done that no amount of resistance could hold back the transformation. The more I tried to fight change, the more I would stunt the emergence of my true self. The paradox was that fighting to remain the me I thought I should be delayed the emergence of the me I was always meant to be. The awakening I experienced led me to find purpose as I wandered through the fires of my life.

Personal transformation comes with a cost. For me it came as a result of racism, shame, guilt, brokenness, introversion, grief, and through absorbing the pain of others. I lacked the knowledge to seek the help I needed. After all, a boy or a man needs to just suck it up, take the thrashing that life throws at him, and keep on ticking. Don't talk about it; don't feel the emotions; don't admit to fear or pain. Trying to understand my feelings is a waste of time. That's what I was told, and that's what I told myself. After all, I am strong; I am fearless; I am without emotion; I cannot be broken. I knew I had better not defy my culture's preordained order of manhood.

Who or what would lead me finally to resolve the cyclical torment that raged inside my mind? Was I alone in the quest of life's fulfillment? How could I let go of a punishing past and move forward? What did tomorrow hold for me? All those questions deserved answers. But my discoveries paled in comparison to the realization that I didn't love me.

Crossing the line from pain to purpose became my transformation to wellness with the help of those who guided and encouraged me to find the peace I so desperately sought. I learned that I could not kick the past out of the car as I drove along the highway of life. Rather, I must embrace the fires of my past to spark the fire of my now. Most importantly, I learned to love myself. All of me. At last, I love the me who lived in a world encapsulated by violence and hatred; the me void of self-confidence who questioned my very existence. I love the me who lived with the false pretense of happiness when, in fact, I was emotionally distraught. I love the me who felt I was never good enough. I love the me who was consumed with loneliness even in the company of others. I love the me who no one knew or understood; the me who searched for acceptance from others rather than from myself; the me who self-inflicted pain to block out the mirror of my life; the me who witnessed friends and family abandon and hurt me. I love me.

The fire of now is my shine to share, it is my duty to teach, it is my honor to give, it is my reason to live. I have found the answers to the two eternal questions: who am I and why am I here? I am a man lit by a fire. I am here to shine my flame of love by giving the best of who I am. In my fire, I carry a mirror to check each morning that what I did yesterday was what I was meant to do. I check the mirror each evening to reflect on what I should do tomorrow. In the mirror, I'm checking to make sure my fire is still lit, still shining, still trying, still leading, and still pleading, not for me, but for all who come in contact with me.

Finally, I am transformed, and my fire now drives me to surrender to inevitable change. I surrender to self-love, self-acceptance, and self-assurance. I surrender to my truth, to who I am supposed to be.

Reflection

In the mirror I see his tears;

He fakes smiles to hide his fears.

In the mirror I see his pain,

trying to hide but hurt just the same.

In the mirror I see his soul,

crushed and cracked, never made whole.

In the mirror I see his hope,

making life more than just a way to cope.

In the mirror I see his dreams,

from pain to purpose, through his screams.

In the mirror I see his shine.

He is special; one of a kind.

In the mirror I see he is real.

Happy or sad, at last he can feel.

Lost are Our Ways

Lost are our ways toward understanding and reconciliation. We are hindered by the insatiable quest to be right as the walls of us-versus-them continue to rise higher and higher. Many are the hypocrites and self-proclaimed prophets of today who speak of good, yet follow evil with no ear for listening and no taste for reason. My path is not your path and yours not mine, but if we should meet on the road of life, may our encounter be empty of the acidity of anger and hatred.

The America of today, like the America of yesterday, will leave an indelible mark on history in its abundance of ignorance, its acceptance of racism, and its suppression of truth. It will leave a legacy of the unfilled promises of "We the people," often replaced with "We the rich," or as WWII Germany called it, "We the Reich," a failed regime of misguided supremacy.

While our earthly lives are confined to the blink of an eye, our history books should be devoid of the unnecessary wars of injustice and filled with pages of purposeful living. The pages of our lives are two-sided. One side records who we truly are, who we have become; and the other side records who we could become. With each passing day, as I turn another page of life, I hope to write a new page, a better page. I can't predict what obstacles will present themselves, but I am undeterred by risk or fear, or even death.

The chapter of my today is filled with pages of activism and faith that press against injustice. The light of right bends the branches of my consciousness and ignites the causes for action in my heart. Saturated with inspiration from the ancestors who struggled before me, I face today with a cup of courage, a bowl of wisdom, and a plate of conviction.

Each day I pray, "Let my words be as strong as steel and my actions be filled with the fire of commitment. When the steel and fire meet, may they forge weapons of mass construction for justice." I accept the batons of activism and faith that have been passed from generation to generation until one day when many are the races that run this race. Activism and faith are forever entangled with insistent persuasion, and the assurance of what is right.

I invite you to name one activist who is not filled with a sense of commitment to something or someone greater than himself or herself. In my case, that someone is God. My faith in God ignites my activism. Both activism and faith are about righting wrongs. Activism involves helping others, and so does faith. Both activism and faith are about reaching deep in your heart and knowing you have been called to do something in this life that leaves a legacy of righteousness. Activism is about making this world better than when we got here, and so is faith. Activism is praying for a better day and so is faith. Activism and faith are not about race. They are about right.

My heart bends firmly toward justice; my spirit swerves sternly toward peace; and my thoughts veer cautiously toward hope. Each day I rise and ask myself, "What shall I do today to make the world better?"

I Have Days

Days of joy,
days of rain,
days of laughter,
days of pain.
It's love I'm after.
Days of storms,
days of light
days of dark
days of strife.
All are the days of my life.
Days I rise,
days I lie,
days I fall,
days I cry.
Every day I still try.

Tears of a Lifetime

A proud and independently strong woman, my mother Odette Cormier, poured courage and love into my cup of life. She sprinkled compassion and perseverance as she served my plate of life. How I would see and hear, how I would think and act, how I would love and hate, how I would naturally nurture the world around me...all were woven into the fabric of my DNA, all were passed on to me from my mother. Intuitively she knew what each of her children needed, fearlessly carrying the torches of education, self-confidence, and determination as her pinnacle values. My mother's siblings, parents, husband, and children each took note of her commands, and her voice demanded a quick and unquestioning compliance. She was the irrefutable matriarch of the family.

Mama's early years were engrossed in becoming an activist, an educator, a writer, and a humanitarian. She fought for justice and was known as a leader in the community, church, and city for raising social and racial awareness and fighting for equality. Her weapon of choice was the sword of education, as she was a prolific reader of various writings of world leaders, activists, philosophers, and well-known clergymen. Her shield in the battle against injustice was God, as she continually uttered words of praise and thanksgiving along with petitions for grace, mercy, and strength. Prayer was a daily habit. Carrying her sword and shield, she entered any arena filled with words of wisdom and conviction that the listeners eagerly anticipated. They knew she would not be denied in her quest for justice. Her nearly six-foot-tall frame, her articulation of both the English and Creole languages, and her two faces of warrior and comforter, would lead anyone who met her to recognize greatness exemplified. Her life of heroism and activism started with less than meager beginnings and continued despite opposition from the people she would fight against and sometimes the people she fought for.

Mama often spoke of growing up on a farm in the backwoods of Louisiana and the hard physical work required by her whole family. She was born in a one-room shack without electricity or running water. They called it *petite cuisine*, Creole for *little kitchen*. Her formative years through high school proved both difficult and motivating.

Mama knew her ticket for a better life could come only through education, hard work, education, determination, education, resilience, education, and education. After completing high school at an all-girls Catholic school, she took on many odd jobs mainly as an indentured servant, cleaning houses and taking care of other people's children. As she recalled those days, tears would follow the stories of pain endured because of racial injustice and pay disparities that typified the unfairness of the times.

It was both a blessing and a curse to work for upper middle class and wealthy families in the South. The curse came in the form of degrading treatment and low pay. The blessings included access to a world of books and exposure to the outside world through observing her employers. Mama consistently praised her creator for the opportunity to earn at least some personal income, money that she would invest in furthering her education. She knew education was the best way to discover who and why she was alive and who she could become.

Eight people lived in our house. There was a bedroom for my mother and father, another for my three sisters, and another that I shared with my brother and uncle. Although we had another room that could have served as a bedroom, my mother made this into what she called the study. Three of the four walls of the study were covered from floor to ceiling with bookshelves filled with books. A round table and four chairs occupied the center of the room. You would have to enter this room with caution as it was sure to change you before your exit. Whether you were an educator, politician, clergy, or drug addict, Mama's doors were open to all for mind bending, book lending, dream sharing, and tear dropping. You could expect conversations of the who, what, and why, along with hearty helpings of her well-known cuisine. No one left our home without eating and hearing a quote from Martin, Malcom, Stokely, Dick Gregory, or one of her own quotes that referenced civil disobedience, self-improvement, or compassion for the under-served.

My mother's favorite activist was Martin Luther King, Jr. She would often recite one of his famous quotes when she was sad, when she was angry, or when she was happy. She could always find the right quote for the situation. When I was in high school, my mother made copies of MLK's famous quote, "Mutuality." It was one of her favorites, and she gave all of the children a copy that she had printed on certificate paper. Each one was protected by a plastic sleeve. I kept the copy she gave me and recently found it in a box I had in a storage unit. I brought it home to look at from time to time as a reminder of the lesson my mother was trying to teach me and everyone else she connected with. Recently my wife, son, and I had dinner with my mom at our house, and I started talking about that piece of paper. As I began reading the quote, she interrupted me after the first three words, and, at ninety years old, recited the quote word for word. It was amazing that all those years later she still had the words burned in her mind. It confirmed to me the importance of the lesson she had taught me almost fifty years prior. Here is MLK's quote, "Mutuality:"

"All life is interrelated. All men are caught in an inescapable network of mutuality, tied in a single garment of destiny. Whatever affects one directly affects all indirectly. I can never be what I ought to be until you are what you ought to be, and you can never be what you ought to be until I am what I ought to be. This is the interrelated structure of reality."

It's not just that my mom had the capacity to recite this quote at her age that impressed me, but the passion with which she delivered it, passion in her voice, her gestures, and her facial expressions. Whenever she told the story of this quote, she explained what it meant to her. When MLK was assassinated in 1968, it was a crushing blow to my mother as it was to many people around the world. Her first plane ride was from Houston to Atlanta to attend MLK's funeral, a trip she wouldn't be denied. His assassination ended his life, but his legacy continued to grow with people like my mother who kept teaching the next generations about her epic hero for racial justice.

As is the case with great people throughout history, my mother was often resented for her tireless work in the community, even by family members, people she considered to be friends, and her church family. The source of resentment came from jealousy, envy, and fear. While the pain sometimes brought her to tears, no amount of criticism would stop her. Rather it motivated her even more to continue. Always the optimist, Mama believed that educating the world to righteousness would someday be met with open arms by everyone, but it was a delusion that caused her to carry the weight of the world's moral compass on her shoulders.

My mother had many strategies to help people. Along with a team of mostly White women, she started one of the first literacy programs in Houston to teach uneducated Black men to read. In 1972 when refugees began fleeing Haiti and coming to the US, many were put in concentration camps. Moved by the injustice of people of color confined to horrific conditions, my mother somehow was able to rescue more than twenty Haitian men. She had them transported to Shepherd, Texas where she and my dad owned a thirty-two-acre piece of land with a house and a barn.

None of the men spoke English. They spoke their native Haitian Creole. But this disparity of language would not be a barrier, as my mom quickly transformed her Louisiana Creole to their native tongue. She would drive an hour one way from Houston to Shepherd every couple of days to deliver cases of fish and other staples for them to eat. The agreement was that these men were to take care of the property and the few livestock there and that they would look for work. She said they could stay until they got on their feet and found jobs. After a couple of months, my parents discovered the men were failing on their end of the bargain, so my father made haste in evicting them off the land and cutting all ties. The reality of what happened with my mother trying to help people who didn't want to help themselves was a blistering blow to her soul that she never forgot.

The '70s brought about many changes, especially in the Black communities across America. While some saw progress in terms of equality for human rights and racial and social justice reforms, my mother saw it as a warning of a false promise. Looking back, I can clearly see how what she was saying then was and still is true today. During my childhood, I was even teased by my neighborhood homies about my mother trying to save the world with her fight for justice and her passion for education. It just wasn't cool back then. That's when I decided I was never going to be like her, helping people, teaching people, learning, fighting for justice, writing, that was not going to be me.

It's interesting to observe how never is often too long to be never. As it turns out, I have become who my mother was in so many ways. The same people who teased me then, the same people who resented my mother and her mission some fifty years ago, and the same people who fought against what she was trying to accomplish, are the people who praise her name today. My mother has wept for this nation, for poor people, for people of color, the incarcerated, the homeless, and every under-served person for the entirety of her life. In her own little ways, she has tried to help them all.

She Wept

She wept when I leaped in her womb,
giving birth in a hate-filled world.
This place that one day would be my tomb,
in her body with stillness, I lay curled.

She wept.

She wept when I arrived,
with hopes and dreams of how I'd grow.
Would they be fulfilled, or had they died?
Letting go, but never letting go.

She wept.

She tried to save an unjust world,
never afraid to speak aloud.
Her trailblazing destiny unfurled;
her path was not followed by the crowd.

She wept.

Physical and emotional pain she wore,
as courage and activism she did preach.
Present and comforting evermore.
Discouraged, but determined, she would teach.

She wept.

Family torn apart, empty of care,
she hoped and prayed for unity.
Discourse far beyond repair,
she was offered no impunity.

She wept.

Aged well, the last one standing.
Queen of the throne for so very long.
Family and friends all gone, she felt stranded,
She wept and wept, till no longer strong.

Now, I weep.

Craig
the Rock

He is My Brother

Ever-present guardian, mentor, guide, debater, athlete, prankster, man of God, thinker, all are adjectives used by many to describe Craig. To me, he wears all those names and many more. He is my brother. A product of private schools, Craig Cormier was one of the first Black students allowed to attend St. Thomas High School in Houston. He was accomplished as both a scholar and an athlete.

Learning came easy for Craig, reading and thinking have always been a passion that propelled his academic accomplishments above the average, but most curricula failed to adequately test his seemingly limitless capabilities. His reading enjoyment was as vast as his intellect. It could be as complex as philosophy and physics or as simple as comic books. His unique ability went beyond reading and comprehending complexity. Craig could, and still can, recall these readings on command and apply them to any conversation. Going to private school and being a thinker became the disconnect between Craig and the neighborhood where there were just as many people who knew him as didn't. Everyone knew who he was, but few people knew the real Craig.

There was a Craig who went beyond the intellectual and athlete, and that was Craig the humanitarian and Craig the rock. I can think of few people I've known in my life who would extend a helping hand more willingly than my brother, and that helping hand was often extended in my direction. He saved me many times. Every family has that one person who takes in people who have reached dark places in their lives, that one person who takes care of the elderly, that one person who will lend an ear, that one person who is the rock of the family. In our family, that one person was Craig, and we all leaned on him. His unshakeable calmness in every situation was remarkable to me and anyone who knew him. Death and grieving didn't shake him, at least outwardly; racism and hate never moved his calmness; war and the possibility of being drafted never scared him. He was just unshakably calm. Craig's intellect and humanitarian efforts were passed from mother to son; his courage and fearlessness came from our father; but that calmness had no apparent roots. Craig didn't just see people and things, he saw through them for what they truly were, nothing more and nothing less.

Craig's view on racism and civil rights had a different perspective than most. He saw racism as not so much a black-and-white issue as a right-and-wrong issue. Craig and I endured similar acts of hatred. Our experiences were different, but at the end of the day, we were both subjected to segregation, integration, racial slurs, hateful actions, and multiple injustices.

We sometimes shared the same viewpoints, but often held totally different perspectives. One thing we shared that still holds true today is that while many injustices came from how Whites treated Blacks, there were also injustices in how Blacks treated other Blacks. We would go to Louisiana and be called "nigger" by Whites and come home to Houston and be called "geechie" by Blacks from Texas. Both slurs represented less-than-human. We were less-than to Whites and less-than to Blacks--the bottom of the bottom of the pot. While this attitude often angered and saddened me, Craig brushed it off without cause for alarm or recognition. My disdain for Blacks was at times equal to my disdain for Whites. At one point, I hated people; I hated myself, but I always loved my brother and his aura of wellness. He knew who he was and what he was; he knew his value in life and his purpose. He was determined to ignore the ignorant.

Craig has had his fair share of battles and his health was one of the battles that would draw him as close to death as one can come. Because of his battle with heart disease and multiple infections, Craig went from a strapping 220-pound man to less than 130 pounds. His body appeared as that of a feeble old man, but he would never discuss his illness, always deflecting any conversation about it. I was crying day and night, worried he would die, but Craig just continued being Craig, unbothered by his condition. I wanted to do something special with him, thinking that his ultimate demise was coming soon.

As life would have it, our family hero of all time, Muhammad Ali, died that year. Craig and I decided to go to Louisville and try to get into Ali's memorial service. With no tickets, we tried every possible way to gain admission. The night before the event we met up with some friends of a friend, people we had never known. One was a state senator with his wife. When we met them in the restaurant for dinner the night before, they surprised us with tickets to the memorial service. We were elated and forever grateful to be able to go to this prestigious and important event. As if that was not exciting enough, after the memorial service, the senator and his wife got us into the private gathering at the Muhammad Ali Center, where only the rich and famous were invited. Here we were two men lacking any repute or fame walking into the center with TV cameras in our faces and celebrities from all over the world. Thousands of people standing outside were roped off and screaming as celebrities entered like they were walking the red carpet, and my brother and I were part of the guest list.

Upon entering, I could barely breathe, but Craig never once seemed awed by the audience or the other guests. He maintained his cool calm self as if he was just hanging out with regular people. To me, it was a story-book fantasy, but to Craig, it was just a walk in the park as he continued teaching me, leading me, and guiding me with every step. My father would always tell us that no man was any better or worse than we were. He encouraged us to walk humbly with respect and to always be fearless. Craig's best friend, William Cunningham, once said, "To truly learn something is to live what you've learned, anything else is merely memorization." Craig lived the lessons he learned and showed me the way.

With Craig's life in the balance, I thought I had given him the trip of a lifetime, my final gift to him. After we returned home, Craig was admitted to the hospital and underwent a risky treatment. Surprisingly, the treatment worked, and he was given a second chance at life. His doctors told him it might keep him alive for three to five years. Craig's health battle returned with the same condition and similar symptoms, and again, he faced it with courage and grace.

While Craig was in this second battle for his life, I, too, fought a battle for my life with a brain tumor. Craig, undaunted by his condition, was by my side daily making sure I was okay. When I was in the hospital preparing for surgery, he came to my side, as sick as he was, to comfort me and reassure me that I would make it through. I made him promise that he would take care of my son and wife if anything happened to me. In turn, he made me promise to fight like hell and make it through the surgery. Craig stayed at the hospital over twelve hours until my surgery was over, and I was in recovery. We both lived up to our promises to each other and both are healthy and retired. Every couple of months Craig and I make a one-day trip to the small towns in Louisiana where our parents grew up. We shop for certain grocery items best found in those towns; we visit the few relatives who are still alive; and we put flowers on the graves of our father, grandparents, and other relatives. But mostly, the trip is for us to get away from the world and enjoy our deep conversations and our favorite companionship: each other.

Now when Craig and I talk about his health issues and what he was going through, he says he didn't—and still doesn't—worry about dying and says it's all part of living. He has always dedicated his life to doing what's right, living right, helping right, and loving right. He has always told me his code for life is in a bible verse, Matthew 6:1 "Be careful not to do acts of righteousness in front of others...." Meaning we all should help one another not for recognition but for righteousness, and that's how Craig lives his life.

A Brother's Love

Beyond memory, beyond love,
my hand in his, fitting like a glove.
Always in front, with me close behind,
his love for family, so real and so kind.
Ever present are his teaching and protection,
his loving kindness I see in my reflection.
A kiss from the stars above all others
I thank God for the best of brothers.

Give Your Last

Life has taught me that we are not measured by what we have in this world. The true measurement of a man is what he gives to this world. It is not the giving from our plenty. Rather it is in the giving from our last that we find our strength and character. My teacher for this lesson was my brother Craig.

In his late fifties, Craig's career proved challenging when he got into a confrontation with a co-worker that would cost him his livelihood. One day he was pushed and hit by this co-worker during an argument. My brother asked the man to stand down, but instead, he hit Craig again. Finally, Craig reached the point of having to defend himself, and a fight ensued. Both the co-worker and Craig were terminated, and, at his age, finding employment became a difficult task. Married with two sons and unemployed, Craig kept his calm demeanor and faithfully continued about the business of being Craig.

At the same time, a family friend, Willy, had become terminally ill with brain cancer. Willy had no place to go, no money or insurance, and he was dying. Even though my brother was unemployed and struggling financially, he took Willy into his home and cared for him for over a year until he died. Who would do that? Well, only Craig, a man lit by faith, friendship, kindness, and compassion.

Shortly after Willy's death, and after Craig's numerous attempts to fight wrongful termination, the company that fired Craig reinstated him. Not only was Craig reinstated but he was given full back pay for the year and a half that he was absent from work. Was this fate, destiny, divine intervention? Was it Willy reaching down from heaven? I will never know, but what I learned from Craig was to always be faithful. Things happen for a reason. Just continue to help your neighbor and be true to yourself no matter the cost.

The Last Twenty-Four

Would I laugh;
would I smile;
would I sing;
would I dance for a while?

Would I watch flowers bloom;
would I feel the wind on my skin;
would I walk barefoot in the grass;
would I be real or just a mannequin?

Would I watch the sun rise;
would I sit with the moon and stars;
would I release my hurt and pain;
would I cast off my emotional scars?

Would I talk with you;
would I uncover my heart;
would I touch you with my words;
would our love for each other never grow apart?

Making the World a Better Place

Aline, a Life of Service

Many, if not most, of my good childhood memories come from my time in Louisiana centered around my Aunt Aline and a one-room house called the *little kitchen*. My childhood summers brought time away from life in the busy city of Houston to a small town called St. Martinville, where my grandparents and two aunts lived off the beaten path. It was there that the sun would kiss my face; it was there that I felt most comfortable, at peace, loved, and happy. The four of them offered an irresistible, caring, and compassionate love. It seemed as though my siblings and I were the only people on earth who mattered because to them we were. Their reclusive lives did not allow for others to enter their thirty-three-acre property, and for the entirety of my life, very few people ever visited. This city boy came to yearn for the simple country living, good Creole food and culture, clean air, fields of various crops, and livestock. On the north, south, and west sides of this property lived relatives: first and second cousins and a great aunt. There was love in every direction, and in the middle of it all was a four-foot-ten-inch woman. Aline, my mother's sister, literally ran from the time she woke till she went to bed.

My two aunts and my grandparents all served their various roles on the farm, working tirelessly from morning till night; but it was Aline who was the spoke in the rim that turned the wheel. All the women cooked, but it was Aline who was in charge of the kitchen. They all cleaned but their tasks were never finished until Aline finished. All cared for livestock, but Aline fed and cared for them the most.

My grandfather was handicapped with physical ailments. My grandmother worked for a rich elderly woman down the road. My other aunt, Lydie, was reclusive with a very soft exterior. That left Aline to bear the heavy lifting, which she did with cheerful grace.

I'm not sure why, but Aline was always running when she was outside. She would run from the main house to the *little kitchen*, her feet seemingly never hitting the ground. Each house had three steps to climb that Aline would fly over and land on the porches. Aline would also run toward the back of the property to feed chickens, pigs, and other livestock in the mornings and evenings. She never stopped running as if she was in a rush to get everything accomplished. Running was just her mode of operation. The only time Aline would rest was after she put everyone to bed and retired to the room she shared with her sister. Aline led a life of service to others and the *little kitchen* served as her throne from which to teach, to learn, to serve, and to love. Aline was part of the *little kitchen*, and the *little kitchen* was part of Aline. Both were woven into the fabric of my life. Aline and the *little kitchen* were my safe haven, where I could cry and release my soul of all the pains and fears of growing up. I didn't even have to utter a word. It was like Aunt Aline and my grandparents could read my mind. Even in silence, they provided the comfort I needed just when I needed it, making life bearable.

Aging was not kind to Aline. She suffered many afflictions, but even through pain, her grace shined the light of hope. My mother, siblings, and I all helped Aline during her final years, serving her as best we could, but our efforts paled in comparison to what she did for us. While we all helped, it was my brother Craig that Aline most connected with and wanted at her side to help with her care. Craig and Aline were alike in many ways, serving other people, practicing their faith, teaching others, and caring for the elderly and children. They had a connection that time could not break and words failed to properly describe.

As death came closer to Aline's doorstep, watching life slowly leave her crushed my soul; but she taught me through faith that she was not fearful and that her reward was waiting in the life to come. Her favorite sayings to all of us were, "God is good" and "Things are going to get better and better." For her these were not just sayings. They were truths, her truths that she lived with and eventually died with. She voiced these two sayings on her deathbed, still serving us, still encouraging us, and still loving us.

Servitude

Smells of homemade biscuits
and fig preserves filled the air.
In a troubled world,
With her there; never a care.

Feeding chickens and pigs
corn she grew in the field.
Thanking her creator
for all things she would kneel.

Always running from place to place
Never rushed and never late;
Cooking every day for everyone,
making sure we all ate.

Holding our hands and listening
as we cried about our pain,
encouraging us to keep
God first and let His love reign.

Always a smile on your face,
fighting off death as it nears.
Never complaining, always hopeful
you left us; I can't hold back the tears.

Gone but never forgotten are
you and the lessons you taught.
Serving, caring, and loving others
were the values for which you fought.

The Little Kitchen

There were two houses on my grandparents' property: the main house, and the *little kitchen*, as we called it. Both lacked the comforts of running water, indoor bathrooms, and air conditioning, and only the main house had limited electricity. The main house had three bedrooms and was used for cooking and sleeping. The *little kitchen* was used for eating snacks, resting during the day, sitting on the porch for conversations, taking baths in a tub used to wash clothes, reading by kerosene lamps, and praying. The *little kitchen* was the birthplace of my mother and her siblings, as going to doctors and hospitals was not an option for a family of reclusive people. It was the twelve-by-twelve one-room *little kitchen* that became my amphitheater where the concert of my life was played on instruments of love, joy, food, thought, and comfort all orchestrated by the maestro, Aline. Sweet was the sound of her music as it caressed me, and, even in pain, brought me joy. It was there that the days seemed long with love and short with worry, long with joy and short with sadness, long with smiles and short with tears. My days were made happy as I played with the livestock and harvested crops, but my best days came with the weekly visit from the St. Martinville Book Mobile.

The book mobile, a library on wheels, was one of the few guests allowed to stop on the property. Once a week it would park under this forty-foot pecan tree that grew at the end of the driveway. We would run to it and climb inside with the excitement of checking out a book for a week that my siblings and I would take turns reading aloud at night. I anxiously awaited these nights to see the excitement on my grandparents' and aunts' faces. They were excited by our ability to read, as if they were embarking on a journey with us in the book. My grandparents had never learned to read or write and could barely speak English. Their native tongue was Creole, but they could understand the words we read, and more importantly, they understood the value of education. They also understood the value of hard work and time. Laziness and wasting time were never written on their schedules.

When Aline died, so did the *little kitchen*. It had been unoccupied and unattended for years, falling apart on that desolate road in Louisiana. Yet, it serves as a reminder of a time and place that brought so many good tastes: the taste of family, the taste of servitude, the taste of joy, and the sweet taste of love. The *little kitchen* offered me simplicity and peace, quieting a noisy world. Aline taught me to lean into hope; she taught me the joy of serving others. Who I am today is greatly influenced by my time with Aline in the *little kitchen*.

Baby Girl

Elegant and smooth have always been the attributes that my sister, Connie, was known for, but fearless and determined make up the cornerstone of who she has become. Connie was the first to pave her path to independence and self-actualization, and, more than any of us, she and my mom were the most alike. Both Mom and Connie have been strong, determined, and unwavering in their journeys of who they wanted to be instead of what the world expected them to be.

Connie courageously stepped out on her own at seventeen years old to go to college. Never looking back, she paved her future the way she wanted it paved. Filled with the spirit of entrepreneurship and creativity, Connie launched several successful enterprises that included a catering business featuring haut cuisine and Creole specialties. Then, she started a very successful human resources recruitment agency.

First graduating from the University of San Francisco, she then went on to graduate from the San Francisco Culinary Institute. Connie armed her toolbox with both business and private enterprise acumen. As she strategically started a recruitment company in the era of booming high tech, the Silicon Valley region became her playground. Her businesses were launchpads for a new world where Connie became an integral influence in the art of dining and fine wine for which she is well known in the bay area. Connie is known by people closest to her as a confidant and encourager. With her mentorship, many of her friends have also become successful. Connie's zest for helping others has extended throughout her life, making everyone in her circle better, including me.

While a parent shouldn't have favorites, the reality is they do, and in our family, my mother's favorite was Connie. I, for one, must admit to feeling jealous of their unique relationship. When they are together, they're like two little girls playing house, free from care and worry just dwelling contentedly in each other's company. They are kindred spirits in the areas of education, social and racial justice, conversation, determination, and mental fortitude. Connie's Saturday-morning routine of going to the farmers market on the bay in San Francisco will always lead to a phone call to me as we catch up on the week's activities and any future plans we may have. Connie, the world traveler of the family, shares detailed descriptions of places and people, different cultures, new foods, interesting sites and pictures. It is as if I traveled with her sharing the experiences and good times.

Although she is my younger sister, Connie is a close friend. Her journey has brought with it a new world from where and how we were raised in Louisiana. Connie's new world includes financial freedom, eating and living well, exercise and physical fitness. Whenever my wife and I visit Connie, she takes us to five-star restaurants where almost all the owners and workers know her and give her special treatment. It is like hanging out with the rich and famous. Since Connie is well-known and respected in the food and entertainment industry, her attendance at any establishment is confirmation of its worthiness, causing others to patronize those establishments. Connie has a vast network of acquaintances in both the bay area and New York, where she nurtures an intimate circle of close friends. Her friends have become her friends for life, her chosen family, and her friends have also become our family, people we cherish, recognizing each other's milestones, birthdays, and accomplishments. Our bond is as close as any blood relatives' connection.

There are so many great things to say about Connie and how she has made her life; and I am grateful for how she helped to form my life. Never once turning her back on me and always lifting me, Connie made me care more deeply about myself. When I wanted to give up, she made me keep going. When I was sitting in darkness, she made me find my light. When I was filled with sadness, she made joy reign on me. When I cried, she made me laugh. When I wanted to die, Connie gave me reasons to live. Connie, the self-made woman, made each of us find a better person inside of ourselves.

Silk

Elegant and beautiful is she,
Ever moving, her spirit free.
Free to come and free to leave
her old life behind, never to grieve.

Many she knows, a few she chose,
Living truth and finding herself, she rose.
Her journey rises and rises through pure will,
Making her way, she never sits still.

She makes me think and makes me fight;
she makes me shine and cast my light.
In my heart I always love her.
I thank God for my sweet sister.

"Sonrise"

My life's trajectory changed significantly when I began to care about others, co-workers, spouse, parents and siblings. But for me, the biggest change in attitude occurred when my son was born. Anticipation and pride, mixed with fear, carried my mind's imagination to dreams of who and what this child would become. I didn't realize that transformation would also be knocking on my door. I was raised in an over-protective household and found myself doing the same thing with my son, with his every step, his every encounter, his every tear and laugh. I was doing everything in my power to ensure that Nick didn't experience the pain I went through. My life became a dedication to him, but like the generation of men before me, I assumed fatherhood meant being a provider and a protector. I fell into the delusion that making money was more important than spending time teaching, loving, and caring for him, that with enough money, I could somehow insulate him from the world's cruelty. My father was the kind of man who would give his life to save his children. We knew it by his words and actions, and so it would be with me. In my heart I know I would give my life for my son because without doubt or hesitation, he is my world, my truth, and will one day be my legacy.

I think every parent could write a book about what not to do in raising a child. That book might have only a couple of sentences on what they think they did right. As I recall my child-rearing days, that is certainly the case with me. Most of us try our best and we learn many lessons along the way, but in raising a child there are no do-overs.

Even though my experience of private school had been disastrous, Bridget and I decided it would be the optimum place for our son. San Antonio Academy, the best private school for boys in pre-k through eighth grade, was the overwhelming choice of the rich and famous in San Antonio, and we would do whatever it took to get him in. The tuition cost was certainly above our financial means, but we would figure out a way to afford our son the opportunity and exposure that the best school the city had to offer. Many times, when I would drop off Nick at school, I would tell him that we might be the poorest family at the school but we belonged, that he belonged. While the Mercedes and Porsches dropping off kids were filled with rich parents, nannies and bodyguards, Nick and I would pull up in my older-model Malibu with all the pride in the world.

Unlike my experiences in private school, Nick excelled academically and was loved by many at the academy. He also found his first love, playing the saxophone, and he enjoyed playing basketball.

"Sondown"

After San Antonio Academy, Nick went on to the next phase of his academic career, entering high school. It was there that he encountered one of his life's biggest challenges. Between his ninth and tenth grades, during a physical examination, it was discovered that Nick had a heart murmur. After visiting several doctors, we were given the diagnosis of the heart disease known as hypertrophic cardiomyopathy. This disease, known as a sudden killer, is the abnormal thickening of the heart. Undetected, it could cause death, and in fact, has proven fatal to many athletes. As Nick and I sat listening to the cardiologist explain what this condition meant--no cure and the possibility of sudden death with high exertion--we were devastated. That night at home Bridget, Nick, and I were consumed with fear and confusion. We began the endless journey of research, hunting for the best doctors, the best kinds of foods to eat, what exercises were allowed, and how we could deal with what we thought was a hopeless situation. Tears poured down the cheeks of my wife and son. Being the man of the house, I tried to be the brave one, but failing miserably, I too cried. That night as he always did, Nick led us in prayer, but instead of the "Our Father," he recited:

> "Now I lay me down to sleep,
> I pray the Lord my soul to keep.
> If I should die before I wake,
> I pray the Lord my soul to take."

This prayer came out of nowhere, or maybe it came out of Nick's soul. Regardless, it pierced all of our souls. Going into another room, I cried, and I cried, not knowing what to do, not knowing how to help, not knowing how to protect my son.

When Nick went to sleep that night, I kept going into his room to look at him. I looked at his sheets, watching for the rise and fall of breath that would give me confirmation of life. To our great surprise, the next day Nick immediately began his own research on health, food, and allowable exercise, all with the determination of making the best of his new-found condition. Thankfully, our network of friends and acquaintances in the San Antonio area included many in the medical profession, and they would help us navigate the tenuous process of finding the best-of-the-best in cardiology. We left nothing on the table when it came to making sure we did everything possible for Nick's life and condition.

Bridget commissioned an artist to do a bible verse in calligraphy for the wall opposite Nick's bed. It read, "Through Him, all things are possible." Every day Nick would wake up to those words, and every day Nick would try to do something to better himself.

Three months after Nick's initial diagnosis, an EKG and ultrasound showed promising results as the walls of his heart were not as inflated as his first ultrasound indicated. Another three months and another EKG and ultrasound again showed promise as his heart continued to improve. This went on for over a year, and with unheard-of results, we were directed to one of the most highly respected pediatric cardiologists in the country for further review. The cardiologist was astounded with the initial tests compared to his current tests and determined that either Nick had been mis-diagnosed initially, or he was a modern medical miracle. His heart was normal!

Was it Nick's determination and his change in diet and exercise, was it a mis-diagnosis, was it because he stopped playing sports, or was it "All things are possible through Him?" Nick taught me lessons in faith, courage and determination, and we have continued teaching and learning from one another. While this experience ended Nick's sports career, it also increased his passion for health and fitness. Today his body paints the picture of wellness and physical fitness. With sports out of the picture, his focus for higher education was unobstructed and his journey to college was the next arena that he would dive into.

"Sonlight"

In the summer between his tenth and eleventh grades, Nick spent two weeks in a class at the University of Michigan. Upon returning, he told his mom and me that U of M was the college he would attend. Knowing how difficult it was to get accepted to this prestigious college, knowing that it was the first time my son had ever visited a college, and knowing the cost to attend this institution, Bridget and I never took our son's aspirations seriously. In his senior year of high school, he applied to various colleges and one of them was U of M. Nick received acceptance letters from most of his applications, but he waited anxiously for a response from his dream college.

Away on a business trip, I was golfing with some colleagues when I received a call from Nick. He was crying. He had received his long-awaited acceptance letter from Michigan. The terms of the university's financial assistance were very limited, and Nick knew that going to this school was cost prohibitive for his parents. As we talked and he continued to cry, I pulled my golf cart over to the side. We prayed together, and then I told Nick to get with his mom, write a letter back to Michigan, and tell them why he would be an asset to the school and community. "Ask for more money," I said. "What do you have to lose by asking?" Nick did ask and got a response. Again I was out of town working and golfing. This time when he called, he wasn't crying. He was screaming for joy. Not only did U of M give him more money, but with the increase in financial aid, of all the out-of-state universities Michigan was the most cost-effective school he could attend. Again, Nick and I taught each other lessons in resilience, faith, and the power of the pen.

Dropping off a child at college is an emotional milestone for most families, and we were no exception with the combination of sadness, joy, and pride in our son. The town of Ann Arbor is a quaint college town that surrounds the university. There are many great restaurants and beautiful architecture, and it is diverse and welcoming. Bridget and I admitted to being envious that our son was going to such a fabulous institution of higher learning and wished we had been afforded the same opportunity. After three days, it was time for us to leave our son to start the next phase of his journey in life. Our last night in town, we took Nick to dinner, and as we sat there, I told him I would give him everything I had for the next four years. I told him that for the next four years, I had his back. "You need it, and I will find a way to provide it. If you want to party for the next four years, then party. If you want to sleep late and chase girls for the next four years, then sleep late and chase girls." I told him that the next four years were his to do with as he wanted, but if I were in his place, I would concentrate on getting an education and obtaining a degree because he had only four years. Not five years, but four years. Not four years and one day, but four years. Period. After that life was on him.

Then I took off the chain and cross that I had worn for over twenty years and gave it to him. I reminded him that I was not a man with a lot of money. I couldn't afford to give him a new car. I couldn't afford to rent him a nice apartment. But I could give him what I had always given him: God. I hoped I had handed down to Nick trust in God, and the values of the will to do and the courage to be that had been handed down to me by my parents.

Nick applied himself and went on to graduate in four years. Attending his graduation with family and friends was one of the greatest moments of our lives, a joyous occasion that we will never forget.

After the ceremony, we all returned home. I sat Nick down and told him I was proud of what he had accomplished, and now it was time for him to prepare for his next step in life, his career. I told him that I had his back for the next three months and that he could do anything he wanted for those three months. He could go out, party, chase girls, drink, sleep late, literally anything he wanted to do for three months. Not four months, three months. Not three months and one day. Well, you get the point.

Nick found a job before his three months were over, and his next dream, living in California, became a reality. He landed a job in San Francisco and found a place to live outside the city in the town of Mountain View. I flew there with Nick, so he and I could get all the furniture and other necessities to start his life away from home. My last day in town, we had lunch together just before I left for the airport, and as we hugged and said our goodbyes, I felt something wet running down my cheeks. Hardened by my upbringing with a father made of stone, I was unaccustomed to crying–a crying man was unheard of in my family–but tears filled my eyes. Happy tears and sad tears dropped like rain. I hurriedly left, not wanting Nick to see me cry. As I think about it now, I realize I missed the opportunity to share an uninhibited emotional moment with my son. Finally, I understand the importance of not hiding from my emotions. I have learned to feel my emotions, try to understand my emotions, and share my emotions with the ones I love. I can never recapture that moment, but in the moments moving forward I now know I can let myself be vulnerable with the ones I love.

Nick worked for a couple of years, went back to college at Vanderbilt and got his masters degree. Now he works for a tech company in the bay area, again making me proud. The greatest part of who we are resides in our children, and to that end, my legacy is in good hands.

"Sonlight"

From the dark, the "son" would shine.
A kiss from heaven, God made him mine.
His fingerprints laced with strength and courage;
feet pressing forward, never discouraged.

He brightens my day and lightens my night.
For him, I'd give everything with all my might.
I taught him; now he teaches me.
From boy to man, how great he has come to be.

His life was stirred but never shaken,
my love for him can never be taken.
The love of a father cannot be undone,
the joy of my life; he is my son.

No Options

He Took Me

Twelve college basketball players from across the country living in the land of enchantment, New Mexico State University, would eventually transform from boys to men and men to brothers. The time was the mid-1970's which meant big afro's, tight shorts, knee-high white socks, and enough trash talking to fill many lifetimes. Every player came with dreams of playing professionally, but most of these dreams were quickly dashed when we realized the best- of-the-best players from high school were merely average in college with little chance of moving to the professional level. Yes, basketball seemed important, but the time we spent together was the most important. We filled our todays as if there was no tomorrow, living each day with reckless abandon. Like a child with a box of chocolate, we could never get enough: enough basketball, enough girls, enough laughter, enough drinking, enough eating, enough money, or enough loving each other. The passing of each year would mean some players left and others came in. My entry in 1975 was both the scariest and most exciting time of my life.

Upon my graduation from high school, I had several basketball scholarships, but I also had earned an academic scholarship, the Worthing Scholarship, which meant I could attend the university of my choosing. One day during my senior year, while driving in my neighborhood, I ran into Coach Weldon Drew, who was one of the most accomplished high school head coaches in the country. Coach Drew not only lived in my neighborhood but had also recently signed up as an assistant coach at NMSU for the following year. When he saw me, he stopped me and asked where I was attending college. I told him I was still weighing my options. It was a quick conversation, and, at the time, I thought it held little significance.

When I returned to my parents' home hours later, I was surprised to see Coach Drew there. As soon as I opened the door, my mother told me that I would be going to NMSU with Coach Drew, and that was the end of me weighing any options. I was not the most gifted basketball player; in fact, I would rate myself average at best. So, going to a major basketball program and having to try out for the team was daunting. I was quick, strong, and could jump, but my shooting skills were lacking. My greatest attribute, not only in playing basketball, but in everything I did, was my heart. I simply tried harder than most, giving my all. My "will to do and courage to be," were at the epicenter of my talent. That life's mantra led me to not only make the team, but also become captain of the team both my junior and senior years. To be a walk-on as a freshman and then captain my last two years was an accomplishment I will always cherish, but it could not have been possible without *The Twleve Plus One*.

My team members and I were welcomed into the homes of many within the community for meals and conversation during holidays when all the other students went home, but we were stuck at school with practices. There were many who took interest in us. Two women in particular, Barbara "Ma" Hubbard and Toni Singh gave all they had to us. Ma Hubbard was the "mother" of all the athletes, always caring, sharing, guiding, providing, listening, and loving us more than any of us deserved, more than we appreciated at the time. Toni was an Indian woman who came to all our home games and practices and would always have her blind nephew with her. At the end of each player's college basketball career, she would write a heartfelt poem and mount it on a plaque. This was her poem to me:

You walked onto our campus, with great outstanding traits,
We recognized your talent, so we locked you inside our gates.

We even liked the way you walked, altho' we thought you'd slip,
But we found it very cute, so that's why we called you "Tip."

You gave yourself your total, you played your heart and soul,
Through tough and hard assignments, to be our leader was your role.

We felt that you could guide us, and really play the game,
For your spirit and full devotion, our Captain you became.

You leave behind a stat, a good challenge for the rest,
Your career field goal percentage of the seniors rates the best.

For your overall performance, you were worthy of the selection,
From outstanding Conference players, as "MVC Honorable Mention."

You helped us to a winning season, 22 won games to be exact,
That earned our slot in the NCAA, your 4-year dream became a fact.

Our true and heartfelt thanks to a dear and honest troop,
For leading us in molding, a strong and dedicated group.

This token is for remembrance of your years at Aggieland,
We all will really miss you, and your great outstanding hand.

Twelve Plus One

The Twelve Plus One, **as** we call ourselves today, is more than twelve plus one. It includes the twelve players from each year, along with the coaches, their families, and the community of Las Cruces, New Mexico who all played a part in shaping us as men. The world around us would stop every time we entered a gym for a practice or game, because to us that's all that mattered in the moment. The coaching staff and community gave us unconditional love, compassion, and guidance, helping us whenever they could. This type of generosity for a Black kid from the South was unheard of. This type of generosity lived in our hearts and because of it, we began having reunions that led to a lot of laughing, a lot of crying, a lot of lying, and serving the community that had given so much to each of us.

In 2019 at one of our reunions, we wanted to honor these two ladies for their outstanding service to student athletes. We awarded Ma Hubbard what we called a "widow's mite" as she gave her all from the heart. Unfortunately, Toni Singh is no longer with us, and her nephew is now in a healthcare facility. Due to his condition, we can't visit him, but our hearts are forever grateful for what both he and his Aunt Toni did for the team. While I mention these two special women, there were far too many other supporters to write about, but their service to the team will never be forgotten.

Ma Hubbard and Aunt Toni taught us about the power of giving, that when we give we not only change lives, but our own lives are fulfilled. Our NMSU team from 1975-1979 went on to create *The Twelve Plus One Heart Foundation* in 2018, an organization that gives less fortunate students financial assistance through scholarships.

The community loved us, and we loved them, but the coaching staff taught us lessons that went far beyond the hardwood floor. Coach Drew who took me to NMSU was like a brother, forever watching me and guiding me down the right path. His mentorship continued for years beyond my time in college. When Coach Drew passed away, he had already written what he wanted in his funeral program, and to my surprise, he said that one of his greatest sports accomplishments was developing me as a player from walk-on to captain and helping to develop me to be a man. Little did I know at the time how significant that brief conversation with Coach Drew my senior year of high school would become. The fact that I happened to be driving down his street when he was outside and stopped me changed my life and the lives of so many others. This experience taught me that in life many opportunities present themselves, but we can easily miss them unless we open our eyes. Coach Drew also taught me to look for the potential in others and that we owe it to the world to help develop and support other people whenever we can. This gift is as important to the giver as it is to the receiver.

Our head coach, Ken Hayes, became my father-away-from-home, always nurturing me with encouragement and lifting me in public beyond any recognition I deserved. Coach Hayes was tough and brutally honest. He could break the players who were not up for the physical and mental warfare that Coach would employ. He respected me as a player because he quickly found out that I was not breakable. Nothing he nor any other player could do would ever break my spirit of giving my all both on and off the court. The life lessons I learned from my mom and dad helped me overcome any skill deficiencies and allowed my collegiate career to flourish beyond expectation.

Coach was also known as a person with the gift of gab who could use words to paint mental pictures. In 2018, at one of our reunions, he told a story about writing to my mother every year to tell her how I was doing in school and on the court. When I returned home to Houston, I told my mom that Coach fabricated a story about writing to her. At that point she stopped me and affirmed that he was telling the truth. Not only that, but she also kept those letters. She was able to find one postmarked 1978 and gave it to me. I keep it with all the letters that are dear to my heart. The letter mentioned my basketball accomplishments and how I was doing in school, but, more importantly, it spoke to the fact that he loved me enough to write to my mother and allay any fears and concerns she may have had about me being so far away from home. Coach Hayes and I continue to speak on the phone regularly. At eighty-eight years young, he still has the gift of gab and continues to be a father figure to me. The other players on the team, even his son, would tease me and say I was his favorite, calling him my "daddy." At the time, I felt embarrassed and would get upset, thinking they were ridiculing me, but today I affectionately call him Dad because he is a dad to me. The lessons I learned from Coach Hayes are too many to list, but the most important was to see the best in people and help them shine their light because their shining is also part of your light.

My time in college was not all rosy. I faced many challenges as an athlete, as a student, and as a person of color. Arriving at NMSU and having to try out for the team was a difficult and humbling experience. Having accolades from an inner-city high school and then coming to an environment where I could hardly keep up was emotionally derogating. Being relegated to sitting on the bench my first year was humiliating, and, at times, I wanted to quit and go home. Thankfully, Mama and Daddy weren't having it. Staying at NMSU was the best thing that could have happened to me, especially with the way things eventually turned out.

Forty-five years since college, *The Twelve Plus One* team is closer than we have ever been. We hold regular reunions, call each other regularly, and take turns sending out daily morning reflections to everyone in the group. Usually, around 4:00 AM the chain of texts starts flying to our phones. It's something I eagerly await as it keeps me centered for the day and centered for my life. What makes our bond unbreakable is not that we once played on a team but that we still gather for reunions. These gatherings have become the biggest lie fests you could ever imagine. We sit around for a couple of days embellishing the past and the present and call each other out on our BS. Usually our get-togethers last for three days, the first day is fun just hanging out and telling lies. The second day we find a community service opportunity at a food bank or a shelter. The most recent service project was at a hospice facility, talking and hanging out with the patients. On the third and final day, we take a trip to a place called A Mountain. This mountain is right outside the campus and has the letter A painted on it. It is a place that was once part of our yearly training where we were required to run a specific trail in a specific amount of time. It represented for us a place of pain and was a breaking point physically for many throughout the years. We go there on the third day of our reunions to share the intimate pains we have endured in our lives. Listening and sharing, we realize that all of us go through traumatic situations. None of us is immune. Telling one story more horrific than the one before, we share and we cry, we share and we hope, we share and we care, we share and we love each other more and more each time. The name, *Twelve Plus One*, was never meant to reference the number of players, rather it was chosen in recognition of the twelve disciples plus Mary as a reminder of how we should live our lives and how we should pour our goodness into the world. Today our team is greater than it ever was when we played basketball because now we play the game of love for all, a game with no losers.

In My
Room

Tick Tock

As a relatively healthy man in my early sixties, I never imagined death would come knocking at my door. Maybe ignoring signals along the way blinded me to this unexpected visitor. My life was always filled with exercise, and I was more physically fit than most men my age, so why would I let a few minor symptoms cause alarm? My symptoms were the occasional nosebleed, headaches, and a few dizzy spells, all of which I thought came with age. I went to my primary care physician regularly and had yearly physicals. Nothing my doctor saw nor any lab results uncovered what I was about to experience. Due to the symptoms, my wife forced me to see another doctor. Now I had two women, my wife and the doctor, pushing me to find answers. My body was telling me what my mind was avoiding.

My new doctor scheduled a series of tests and instructed me that if I had any dizzy spells to immediately go to the hospital. I tried arguing with her--I thought going to the hospital for a dizzy spell would be a waste of time--because these spells lasted only a couple of seconds. Of course, a man arguing with a woman is a lost cause, so I complied with her request.

A couple of weeks later, the night before my sixty-second birthday, my son came to town and both he and my wife were taking the birthday boy to dinner. As I drove to the restaurant, I got hit with a dizzy spell and immediately pulled the car over to the side of the road. As usual, in the few seconds it took me to pull the car over, my dizzy spell was over. I wanted to continue on our way to dinner, but Bridget and Nick forced me to go to the hospital as my doctor had instructed.

In an emergency room on a Saturday night in a major metropolis like Houston, it takes hours to get examined by a doctor. When I finally got in, my blood pressure had reached an alarming level, and they immediately administered medicine to get it under control. Over the course of several hours, my blood pressure came down, and although it was still high, I was released from the emergency room to go home.

It was after midnight by the time we got home, and my birthday dinner was obviously canceled. We all went to bed, but around three in the morning, I woke up and sat on the edge of the bed. I told Bridget something was wrong, that I felt really bad, and she did the wifely-doctor-thing and told me I probably just needed to go sit on the toilet and poop. I followed her suggestion.

As I sat there, out of nowhere I felt something overwhelming my body as if I were about to lose consciousness and die. I yelled for help. Bridget and Nick rushed into the bathroom and put a cold towel on my forehead. That's when my eyes rolled back in my head and I became unresponsive...or so they told me later. As Nick was crying over me and holding the cold towel on my head, Bridget went into the other room to call for an ambulance. All of a sudden, I was above my body and could see, from several feet away, my son holding the towel on my head and I could see me. I could hear my wife talking on the phone in the other room as if I were in both places at the same time. I could see with no eyes, and I could hear with no ears; I was gone somewhere but still there with them. As they approached full-panic mode, I watched them and I watched me, but this me floating above it all, outside my body, was calm and never worried. It was as if I were watching a movie about myself. I was nothing, but I was part of everything. Consumed with a warm peace, somehow I knew that no matter how it ended it would not be the end.

Then I felt something wet hit my face and when I looked up, I was back in my body. Nick stood over me crying, and his tears were what I felt. I'm not sure if I died, but I certainly had an out-of-body experience that changed my life and changed how I thought about death. The EMTs entered our home and took me to a second hospital. All of this happened within a twenty-minute time span but for me it was as if only a couple of seconds had passed.

After I was admitted to a hospital, more tests were run and this time a CAT scan revealed that there was a mass in my brain. As the ER doctor explained my condition and the next steps to my wife and me, I could no longer hear what she was saying. All I heard was that I had a mass inside my brain and I might die.

Falling

My family and I had not slept all night, so after a couple of hours, I sent them home. When they left I began to cry uncontrollably with the thought of death looming just over the horizon. The nurses at the nurses' station heard me and came in, trying to calm my nerves, but tears ran just the same. I thought about all the things I had done in my life, but mostly I reflected on all the things I hadn't done. I decided if life would give me another chance, I would do all those things and so much more. I was determined to never look back and regret not doing what I was meant to do. I would not let life get in the way of living intentionally, living purposefully, living fully.

At the same time, I began swimming in the ocean of self-pity, wondering why this was happening to me. After all, I had changed my life and now was doing good work with a foundation I helped create, volunteering with underprivileged kids at a nonprofit, and working for another nonprofit that helped troubled young adults who were incarcerated. I mentored people across the country at various companies where I had worked. I was a member of my church's parish council; I worked with Target Hunger, giving food to the less fortunate; I led a daily church prayer call; I visited the sick in my neighborhood and church; and I had done community service at various organizations around the country.

Looking back at all this now, I guess I had turned into the person my mother was, the person I said I would never be. Surely with all the good I was doing, the universe owed me. But then I realized that bad things happen to good people, too. I also thought about who I would want in the room if I were to die. This question provoked thoughts of those who have gone before, those who are in my life now, and those I will never know. The value of legacy moved from being in the top ten of my life chart to number one.

The following day at sunrise, I was looking out the window of my hospital room, and all I could think about was that I would never leave that hospital, and my feet would never touch the ground again. I don't know why, but this thought ate at me, and when Bridget returned to the hospital, I asked her to walk with me. I didn't tell her what I was thinking, but I knew that if I could get outside I would live again.

When my feet hit the ground outside the hospital, it was my assurance of hope that I would overcome the battle before me. Just a few steps outside inspired all the hope I needed to move forward with determination. After all, I was that kid who was taught "the will to do and the courage to be," and my unbreakable spirit would not allow me to give up or give in.

In the coming months, the search for a neurosurgeon proved successful, and one of the best doctors in the world in Houston Medical Center removed the tumor that was sitting on my pituitary gland. The road to recovery proved tough, and the next days in the hospital were excruciating. Bridget stayed by my side five days in a row post-surgery until I was finally able to convince her to go home and get some rest.

That first night by myself in the hospital I received a visitor. Death came knocking at my door again. Watching TV in my room, I began feeling bad, almost like the night when I had lost consciousness. I felt frightened that something bad was about to happen and called for a nurse. I also called Bridget and asked her to return to the hospital. After I explained to the nurse how I felt, she checked all my vitals and tried reassuring me I was okay, but I was persistent that something was wrong. Like Bridget had said the night of my first attack, this nurse told me I probably just needed to go to the restroom and poop, so I went. While sitting there, I felt death's touch for the second time and immediately hit the panic button. Just as the nurses came into my room, Bridget arrived, and I began losing consciousness. Again, I could hear and see, and again, peace covered me. The medical staff and my wife were screaming my name and trying to revive me, and all I could do was watch them and watch me. After a few minutes, I regained consciousness. The doctors that night and the next day could never figure out what happened to me, but for the second time, I felt death calling, I felt peace comforting, and I felt something in me that was beyond the shell of my body. I felt my spirit.

∫weetness

After a week in the hospital, I was released. I went home thinking that I was getting well and all of this trauma was behind me. Little did I know that the trilogy of death was not done with me. Now my recovery from the surgery was rapid, and I was doing exceptionally well until one day I noticed I was losing weight. I began weighing myself every day and told Bridget of my concern. She tried convincing me that weight loss was part of post-surgery and reminded me that I was eating well every day. But as the days passed I lost more weight, and for me it was noticeable not only on the scale but also in the mirror as I saw my gaunt face.

One night I weighed myself right before bed and again when I woke up, and I had lost three pounds while I slept. Even though I had been back to the doctor for a checkup and blood work, I knew something was not right.

One morning I was feeling bad and decided to go back to bed when my phone rang. It was an unfamiliar number, so I didn't answer. Immediately the phone rang again, and again I ignored it. Then I heard Bridget's phone ringing. She answered the call, and it was the lab that had processed my blood tests. They were calling to tell us to get to the hospital immediately because the lab work revealed that my sugar levels were off the charts. I wasn't diabetic and didn't realize that the steroids I was given post-surgery were causing anomalies in my body. I threw on a t-shirt and some shorts, and we were off to the hospital again.

Bridget dropped me at the front door of the ER and went to park. When I walked in, three nurses were sitting at the nurses' station. I told them I had received a call from a lab, that my sugar level was above 300, and that I was feeling bad. They all looked at me as though I was crazy, and one nurse asked if I had regular bowel movements since my surgery and if not, maybe I just needed to go to the restroom. Okay, now I can see the trend. All three times when I think I'm about to die, a woman thinks I'm full of poop. When they tested my sugar level, it was higher than the machine could register so they immediately admitted me. Thankfully, I hadn't gone to sleep at home that morning because I was told that I could have slipped into a diabetic coma and died.

Almost dying three times in a six-week period taught me many lessons. It taught me that humans are frail, and we should always listen to our bodies. It taught me that time is short, and we must do the things in life we are called to do to leave a legacy. It taught me that there is something beyond this life; we don't just die and it's lights-out; more accurately, we die, and it's lights-on. When our time comes, we will see, we will hear, we will move, we will find peace, and we will know that we are part of something greater than ourselves. It taught me that it's not what we have in this world, it's what we give to the world that's important. Finally, it taught me to ponder who is really important in my life, who has inspired me to imagine and write, and who I want in my room when I die.

In My Room

If I were dying, who would I want in my room? I see my mother and father holding life lessons, waiting for me with smiles. I see my elementary teacher greeting me with a smile and a book. I see my friend, Hillbilly, waiting with a basketball. I see Mrs. Bentley and Coach Hayes who taught me to write and fight. They are standing there with pen and paper and tenacity. I see Muhammad Ali and Malcom X, my heroes, holding courage, faith, and justice. I see my friend, Suryc, who took his life. He is standing in my room telling me it was not my fault and encouraging me to forgive myself. I see *The Twelve Plus One* laughing and telling lies about how great they were but still loving and caring for me. I see my brother Craig and my sister Connie sitting there still encouraging and pushing me to continue fighting. I see my wife Bridget and my son Nick holding me and loving me to the end. There are many others waiting for me in my room; some I know and some I don't. My room is filled with their love, patience, forgiveness, and kindness.

There is a good Cyrus and a bad Cyrus in my room. The bad Cyrus who I once thought was that cool guy who wanted everything at any cost and wanted it all immediately. The bad Cyrus gets kicked out of my room before I die. The good Cyrus, the me I only began to know later in life, is invited to stay... the Cyrus who is filled with hope and passion to do God's will. I realize the good Cyrus was always the real me. I just had to find him. The good Cyrus shows me around the room, introducing me to the people who gave me life, the people who taught me to think well, write well, fight well, be courageous, have faith, seek justice, forgive myself and forgive others, and let go of the bad and embrace the good.

Finally, the good Cyrus shows me the fire. The fire is the Light and the Light is the fire. I hold the Light, and the Light holds me, and somehow I know that the Light is great. The fire is the Light, and the Light is the fire, and the people in my room are part of my fire, and that makes them part of the Light. The fire is bright and so is the Light, and now I can see my room is part of a mansion that the fire and Light have built for me. The fire and the Light are my all-in-all, my everything. My fire bows to the Light, for my fire knows that the Light is Him. The fire and the Light are in my room; the fire and the Light are in me, and I am now in them. When the time comes, who do I want in my room?

I want the fire and the Light.

Grace
Under Fire

Be Who You Need to Be

Life has taught me that being the real me is being the me of many, the many I could be. I learned to be a different me, a changing me, a transformative me, a me of today, a me of tomorrow, a me of now, and a me of later. This lesson was taught to me by my mother and her ability to be chameleon-like, depending on what the situation and people in her life needed at any given time.

My mother was multi-dimensional in her pursuit of making this world a better place. Mama would one day entertain city and state activists for racial justice. The next day it could be White women discussing women's rights and social justice. The next day it might be clergymen and clergywomen of different faiths in discussions about spreading and living the word of God. Another day Mama would regale kids from the neighborhood with stories from her past as well as the state of current affairs and how Black people could move forward. In our home, the range of people and discussions was limitless. At times it felt like our home was a school, a board room, an office, a confessional, and a church, all with my mother as the leader.

See Me

See me, not him.
He wipes away tears;
I rise out of brokenness.
See me.

He rejects the mirror;
I embrace the reflection.
See me.

He runs from fear;
I hold on to courage.
See me.

He is gone; I am here.
See me.

Run to Serve

"Service to others is the rent you pay for your room here on earth."
Muhammed Ali

We are all born to serve but the choice is ours. It is in our eagerness to serve (run to serve) others that the foundation of creation is built and continues to grow. My Aunt Aline taught me the importance of serving others.

Aline ran and ran but time would catch up to her. When she became the last of the four family members to be living, my mother didn't want her to be alone, so she moved Aline to Houston to live with her. Since Aline had traveled outside the town of St. Martinville only once in her lifetime, moving to Houston was monumental for her. At sixty-one years old, starting over in a new place would have proven difficult for most, but time could not hold her down. For Aline, her north was true, and serving others remained her mission in life. Her tireless work continued.

Although Aline had never been a TV person, she somehow became infatuated with watching golf, and, in particular, Tiger Woods. She had never seen a sporting event, had only watched a couple of soap operas, but she was now a golf fanatic. She would call me and ask if I was watching a tournament that Tiger was playing. She would recite the score and give me a play-by-play commentary of his shots. She knew how much I loved to play golf and would say that I would one day play a round with Tiger. Well, that never happened, but it was her way to encourage me as she always did with everything I pursued.

At my mother's home, Aline took over the majority of cooking, cleaning, and caring for my siblings' children who lived in Houston. She also became the primary caregiver for her two brothers who lived in the same neighborhood, cooking all their meals. Aline served three generations: parents, siblings, nieces, and nephews, then great nieces and nephews, all without complaint. It was just what she loved to do.

Purpose Found

Thoughts of peace
from the heights of
giants before me,
I too imagine a world
of what could be.
From the cray cray
of this mad, mad place
that I lay lay,
I stop and pray pray.
Guiding my thoughts,
transforming my journey,
pushing my path from
straight to crooked
then crooked to straight.
my feet peddle toward
the untrampled ground,
making first footsteps
that last as I plant the
prints of goodness
that billow inside of me.

Lifted in Love

The greatest innate human emotion is to love and be loved. Time and space cannot contain love and love can never end. My sister Connie taught me to lift others in love.

Like my mother, Connie took particular interest in my well-being when we were children and extended this caring for me into adulthood. Her lifelong belief is that, while we are all the same, we are each unique and that good people are good no matter who they are. Connie never let race, gender, sexual orientation, age or anything else come between her and the possibility of building a relationship of trust and respect with a person of good heart and character.

While I was in college in New Mexico and she in San Francisco, she would write me letters, always checking on me and encouraging me to do well in academics and athletics. She was and is my personal cheerleader for life, wishing me well, pushing me well, and loving me well. Whether it was her intention or not, each of her letters contained a subtle message encouraging me to strive for excellence and always help the helpless. Also embedded in those letters were her views of acceptance of all people regardless of the stereotypes the world puts on them. We don't write letters anymore. Rather, we send texts and emails. But we have always made time to talk on the phone and visit each other in the various cities where we have lived, just to share a precious moment of love between a brother and a sister.

Love Never Ends

I rise above the clouds;
I sit with the stars.
The light of the moon
shines through my soul.
From my soul to my spirit,
the fire of my life is
still burning, still yearning.
The kindling of love
releases sparks that fly,
to be caught in
some distant land,
in some distant time,
to catch fire once again.
Love never ends; it only begins.

Boiler
Room

Timeless

It would take another book to uncover and unpack the life Bridget and I have had starting as young teenagers and continuing through forty-one years of marriage. I would like to take partial credit for our union of these many years, but with an honest look in the mirror, all I can see is the reflection of Bridget and her loving heart and giving spirit. She is the glue that has kept us together. We went from puppy love, to hot love, to mad love, to crazy love, to quiet love, to angry love, before landing on real love. Growing up, we lived in the same neighborhood, went to the same school and the same church. Even our mothers had attended the same school in Lafayette, Louisiana decades earlier. I was the basketball player and Bridget was the cheerleader. Growing up some nine blocks apart, we have known each other our entire lives.

With all the similarities we were still perfect polar opposites, Bridget the extrovert and Cyrus the introvert, Bridget the romantic and Cyrus the realist, Bridget the extrospective and Cyrus the introspective. But at the core, both Bridget and Cyrus were and are givers. Her mother died when Bridget was twelve years old. As the oldest, she helped her father by taking over many of the household duties. Assuming that role at such an early age conditioned her to be nurturing, loving, and giving. I, on the other hand, grew up with a mother in the home who was a giver to not only the family but to everyone she came in contact with. She conditioned me to be a giver. Loving and giving run on parallel tracks; you can't have one without the other. It is at the intersection of loving and giving that Bridget and I meet and that is what binds us eternally.

Our journey appeared storybook to the naked eye, but like all relationships, the emotional roller-coaster was ours to ride. Unlike many couples, we figured a way to ride the ride and come out on the other side. The loneliest number is one; the toughest number is two, but somehow Bridget made two perfect. The times I was absent she was there; the times I was lonely she was there; the times I was in pain she was there; the times I wanted to give up she was there; the times I was dying she was there; the times I grieved she was there; the times I fell she was there; and the times I rose she was there. Every time I needed someone, she was there just in time; she is timeless.

The lessons I learned from marriage are many, but the few I cherish and try to always remember are:

- Laugh like children, love like teenagers, listen like your life depends on it.
- Life's journey has separate footsteps; don't step on each other's toes.

- We can see things differently, and it's okay to be different.
- Keep a short memory; you both will screw up.
- Have boundaries, but stay close.
- The perfect marriage can never be perfect as long as you are in it.
- The tongue is the most dangerous weapon in a marriage.
- If it's not going to matter a hundred years from now, let it go.
- Give your all, love your all, be your all.
- Be kind, be gentle, be grateful, be timeless.

Bridget is a humanitarian like my mother, always trying to save the world from itself, trying to save people one person at a time, trying to save me from me. Forever casting her net of kindness and generosity, Bridget is known throughout the many cities and communities where we have lived, as a messenger of goodwill. Her love of people is a magnet that instantaneously draws out the love in me, the goodness in me, the kindness in me, and compassion from me. How Bridget didn't give up on me when I gave up on myself, I will never know nor understand, but I will always be grateful. She is my love and my joy in this life.

I have captured each phase of our journey in verse:

She Sees Me

She sees me, and I see her.
Her fire is lit,
calling for my surrender
to embrace the once-was
to the once-is
to the once-will-be.
Her touch is the scratch
of the match
that lights my fire.
Two fires become one,
one that grows and never dies.

Here I Come

I knock on your door,
and you let me in.
I come to court with blind love,
your father with the eagle eye
watching my every move.
He knows our love;
he keeps you safe,
keeps us safe as our love grows.
He's been there, and he knows.

Forgiveness

I broke your heart;
you cried and said good-bye,
never to be together again.
Never is too long to remain forever.
You surrender to me once more
with tears, joy, and love.
I learn and break no more.

Creation

*A child comes and
our joy explodes.
Life changes when we
are childless no more.
We do our best with little.
In return we receive much more
than we could have imagined.
Our love together,
made love whenever,
is now love forever.*

Moving in Place

*We moved from place to place,
city to city, and there
you made each house a home.
Living with you each day
was Christmas for me;
my gift from heaven I could see.
The only real move was
our hearts moving closer each day.
Now two hearts are one.*

When

When I fell, you lifted me.
When I cried, you comforted me.
When I rose, you raised me higher.

When I dance, your feet I see.
When I speak, your heart listens.
When I don't speak, you still hear me.

Comfort and Pain

In the passing of family and friends,
holding each other, our hearts mend.
Grieving and not breathing,
I breathe for you and
you breathe for me.
You give the breath of life;
I give breath back to you.
You are my breath of life.
You are me, and I am you.
We are one, no longer two.

You Saved Me

I lay still and you rescued me;
my lifeless body you could see.
Never worried, you held me
close in your arms.

Your whisper woke me,
and again I rose.
My eyes opened, and you were there,
caring for me once more.

Our journey, nearly shattered,
is still a journey
because you were there,
and you remain.

I Step

I step courageously without hesitation.
I step holding conviction without fear.
I step ferociously with all my might.
I step for the one who holds my heart.
I step with the one who's in my heart.
I step knowing our love will never part.
I step with you and for you.

Forever

Our life has come full circle
from where we started.
We stand changed and
yet the same.
We grew and we aged;
All the while our love could not be caged.
We learn and we teach,
lifting each other through the breach.
A lifetime of love still going strong,
Our strength is forever,
and forever's not long.
When our time on Earth expires,
our love will remain because
you are my love; you are my fire.

A Lifetime of Love

We were just kids when we fell in love,
Athlete and cheerleader, we fit like a glove.
A life together we would build;
hard work in marriage one must till.
Till the soil and till the soul,
never letting our hearts grow cold.
I failed you, but you lifted me.
You prayed and our love is now free.
Four decades later our lives still on fire,
My love for you will never tire.
In this world you are what I most desire,
You are my strength; you are my fire.

What Did I Miss?

Consumed with work, exhausted from trying to make a living, relentlessly acquiring the things of this world, I spent too much time hanging out just to hang out and sleeping way too much. Too often captured by TV and any number of other distractions to pass the time, what did I miss?

I carried a mental list of values that I told myself were the most important things in life, but now when I take stock of how much of my life I invested in those "important" things versus how much time I invested in the truly important, I realize my priorities were out of balance.

Faith and religion were too often one-hour Sunday-only experiences to make me feel good. Family consisted of the occasional few days when I was home and not working, Friday evening through Sunday night. I was consumed by the business of the world, leaving little time for the business of togetherness. The rare occasions of going to dinner or meeting friends for drinks at restaurants or to each other's homes offered little opportunity to grow what could have and should have been lifelong meaningful relationships. Service, elevating myself on a platform of Mother Teresa's goodness manifested in a once-in-a-while food line or donating a couple of canned goods to a food bank.

Truth danced in and out of my existence, but mostly, I was lying to myself. Truth was the ever-elusive holy grail that I had searched for the entirety of my life. It would appear then vanish in the blink of an eye. Legacy, not what I have acquired in this world but what I have given to this world, was nonexistent. The easiest person to fool was the fool inside of me; the hardest person to fool was the man in the mirror who I all-too-often avoided.

Faith, for me, is believing in something greater than myself. Most of my life, I missed the holistic meaning of faith, thinking it meant only believing in God and his teachings. What about the faith of believing in others, the faith of believing in eternal time, the faith of believing in a nation, the faith of believing in relationships, the faith of believing in self, the faith of believing in love; what about that faith?

My early life was filled with others letting me down and me letting others down. I wanted to dwell in the now with all the self-gratification I could get. I wanted to be happy; I wanted things; I wanted love…I, I, I. To be fair, I was not alone in my selfishness. Our nation has reared its ugly head with its constant struggle of left-versus-right, each side with no regard for the other. We argue about abortion, gun control, voters' rights, immigration, economy, infrastructure, health care, and so many other issues with no desire to understand the other side's view. I can drop you and you can drop me, and neither will lose sleep. So I must ask myself, "Do I really have faith or am I just faking it till I make it?

Faith--believing in something greater than myself--was for most of my life, nothing more than me kidding me. Faith for me today is doing, giving, and loving with what little I have to make a difference in my lifetime. That's faith. For years I missed faith, but now I have it.

Then there's love. Our greatest yearnings as humans are to love and be loved, and somehow most of us are in constant search of it. Family is love with an unwavering commitment and resolve to do whatever is necessary to protect, provide, comfort, make glad, lift to the sky, and have no regrets. Family is not always blood and as the saying goes, "we can't choose our family," but true family is who you choose. Sometimes I choose a blood relative, sometimes I choose a friend, sometimes I choose a stranger, sometimes I choose the homeless and forgotten, sometimes I choose the underserved, sometimes I choose church members, but always I choose me. I am the most important person in my family to me and after I choose me, then I can choose you.

Friends are close friends, distant friends, friends of acquaintances, friends at work, friends for a while, but real friendship is forever, friends who become family. Friends can make tears, friends can make laughter, friends can make mad, and friends can make glad, and true friends will always make up. I've lost lots of friends, and only a couple of them remain forever in my heart. They have become family. I missed friends because I didn't know how to be a friend, but now I understand that friendship, like conversation, is a two-way street. I must extend myself to you if you are to extend yourself to me.

Service to others is our willingness to be selfless in action for no other reason than to help those who need help. I didn't always serve; most of my life I wanted others to serve me. I was always hungry for something until I stopped taking and started serving, and that's where my hunger became satisfied. I am full when I give of myself; I am full when I lift the lowly; I am full when I wipe the tears of the hopeless; I am full when I step out of me and step into others.

Truth can be suppressed, but eventually the light of truth will rise and be revealed. I have run from, hidden from, hurt from, and grieved from my truth, but finally I summoned the courage to face my truth. I can no longer continue to bury my past; it will forever be a part of me, but I can bury the pain from my past and let it fade to dust. I can bury my rejection of self and walk hand-in-hand with my truth. I can bury guilt and shame and step forward into the season of self-assurance. I can take hold of my past as my power, shake off the dust of sadness, and live in the light of happiness. I can bury the broken parts of me and let faith and fire glue me into wholeness. I can bury the darkness in me and be filled with light as I continue wandering through the fire. I want a better world, and that means making me a better me. It means paying the heavy cost of authenticity, vulnerability, acceptance, forgiveness, and compassion. Every day I must strive to find my truth, live my truth, and be my truth. Many days I fail, some days I succeed, but everyday I try.

Hope is seeing the unseen, believing the unbelievable, and trusting without reservation. This is the hope I missed as a child. All I could see was the hate in this world with no future of better days to come. I missed the hope of kindness, the hope of togetherness, the hope of understanding, the hope of inclusivity, and the hope of trust. Today I stand with the armor of hope shielding as many as I can shield, knowing that the vision in my mind of unity and peace can be realized. I take hope when I rise and when I die, for without hope, I am nothing. Hope is my rod and my staff that guides my footsteps along the path of life, and I share my hope with others as many people have shared their hope with me. I pray my grip on hope never loosens as I carry the torch of hope to keep my fire burning,

Legacy, for me, is all the good that I've poured out into the world; and if I'm not empty when I leave here, then I failed. I would have failed you and I would have failed me, but there is hope that with each passing day, I drip a little more of me into the pool of humanity. Too often I have missed the chance to leave a worthwhile legacy, but today I release all that I have to give, to be passed from one person to the next. I drip a seed of patience and pour myself where it counts. I drip a seed of empathy and pour a little understanding. I drip a seed of favor and pour a giving spirit for someone to hold hope. When I die, I hope my drips become ripples in the lives of others, ripples that answer the question of why I was here.

Now I ask myself, "What did I miss in this lifetime?" More importantly, "What have I given back in this lifetime?"

The Fire to be Continued...

For now, my fire is still lit with the lessons I have learned, and I press forward bathed in self-healing, rinsing off the troubles of the past with the hope of tomorrow. From small fire to raging fire, from painful fire to comforting fire, from the fire of despair to the fire of hope, my fire burns on. Fire has many names: conscience, spirit, soul, love, ego, shame, guilt, pride, pain, purpose, passion, and greed, but for now I call my fire, "Shine." Every day that I rise I can either leave the wick unlit or light my "shine" for the world to see. I can let it burn me or comfort me; I can try to hide from it or let it reveal my identity; I can let it imprison me or set me free; I can let it lie to me or find my truth in it. Today I choose to rise as these lessons continue to grow the "shine" inside of me. Wandering through the fire has taught me to forgive myself and find my authenticity.

At the epicenter of the battle of life is the battle of self, forever doubting, forever ashamed, forever guilty, and forever unforgiving...not forgiving others and, more often, not forgiving myself for things I've done and things I haven't done. For many years, my battle with self failed to produce a winner. I was always the loser. A wall stood between me and moving forward in life, a wall that I couldn't walk around, climb over, or dig under. I discovered that I could break through the wall only with the power that forgiveness unleashes. Learning that I am perfect with all of my imperfections was my first step toward self-forgiveness; and self-forgiveness was my first step toward self-acceptance. Today I can accept myself for who I am, working on my inadequacies and leaving behind my past. Today I dare myself to forgive myself, I dare to be me.

Dare I

Dare I laugh, dare I smile?

Dare I sit and stay awhile?

Dare I care, dare I cry?

Dare I live fully, dare I try?

Dare I do, dare I be?

Dare I accept just being me?

Dare I love me, dare I love you?

All these dares, I dare to do.

Acknowledgments

This book and my life are made possible with inspiration, help, and love from:

Odette Cormier
Joseph B. Cormier
Connie Cormier
Craig Cormier
William Cunningham
Lynn Underwood
Weldon Drew
Craig Wiltz

The Twelve Plus One:

Ken Hayes	Betty Hayes
Ken Hayes Jr	Rhonda Drew
Donald Dotson	Gil Williams
Robert Gunn	Greg Webb
Notie Pate	Dave Brunson
Chuck Goslin	Slab Jones
Richard Robinson	Mark Temple
Micah and Elijah Owens	Phil Elders
Bill Myers	Ernest Patterson
Randy Burge	Louis Saucedo
Randy Moose Gomez	Nicole Gomez
Barbara "Ma" Hubbard	Shari Jones

Brian Colon and the *Albuquerque Men's Group*

Jeanne Johansen, Owner, Cindy Freeman, Editor,
High Tide Publications, Inc.
all the other Authors and Administrative Support at High Tide

About the Author

Cyrus M Cormier

"The measure of a man is not what he accumulates in the world; a man's true measure is what he gives to the world." Cyrus

Cyrus Cormier, is a father, husband, writer, poet, speaker, mentor, and activist. Now a retired executive, he is focused on writing about legacy, social/racial justice, religion, spoken word, and poetry. Author of two books in his fire trilogy, *Wandering Through the Fire* (volumes 1 and 2), Cyrus reveals his life's journey while expressing gratitude to all who helped him along the way. His goal is to give others hope and inspiration so they, too, can demonstrate resilience and perseverance while overcoming adversity.

Cyrus completed his Bachelor of Arts degree from New Mexico State University, where he was a student athlete. His experiences as a leader on the basketball court helped him craft his skills in the business world and in his various post career endeavors. He later went on to complete executive leadership education at Vanderbilt University. During his career, he amassed a collection of best-in-class awards at various corporate entities where he excelled at all levels.

In his spare time, Cyrus enjoys helping his neighborhood and city fight air and ground pollution. He also works in hurricane disaster relief planning and flood mitigation in the Houston area. He serves as President of the *Twelve Plus One Heart Foundation*, where he dedicates his time in fundraising and awarding college scholarships based on financial need. Cyrus works on a variety of other civic and church initiatives that include fighting environmental injustices and helping to provide for the underserved.

Made in the USA
Middletown, DE
19 March 2022

62911833R00052